Crafting
Springtime Gifts

25 adorable projects featuring bunnies, chicks, lambs and other springtime favourites

Copyright © Cappelen Hobby, Norway
Originally published in Norway as *Påske Med Tildas Venner* by Cappelen Hobby in 2004

First published in the UK in 2006 by
David & Charles
Brunel House Newton Abbot Devon
www.davidandcharles.co.uk
David & Charles is a subsidiary of F+W (UK)
Ltd., an F+W Publications Inc. company
Reprinted 2007, 2008 (twice)

A catalogue record for this book is available from the British Library.

ISBN-13: 978-0-7153-2290-1
ISBN-10: 0-7153-2290-7

Paperback edition published in North America in 2005 by KP Books,
an F+W Publications Inc. company
700 East State Street, Iola, WI 54990
715-445-2214/888-457-2873
www.krause.com

A catalog record for this book is available from the Library of Congress: 2005929428

ISBN-13: 978-0-89689-256-9
ISBN-10: 0-89689-256-5

Printed in China by SNP Leefung Printers

Preface

Easter and springtime

It was decided in the year 325 that Easter Sunday should fall on the first Sunday following the first full moon after the spring equinox. We therefore celebrate Easter some time between 22 March and 25 April. An early Easter will sometimes remind you more of winter than springtime, but Easter is traditionally a celebration of spring, with eggs and bunnies as symbols of fertility and new life.

The name Easter was derived from a much older pagan festival held for the goddess Eostre who was the Anglo Saxon goddess of spring and the sunrise. Her symbols were the hare and the egg for fertility. Today we give each other Easter eggs and hide eggs in the most unlikely places for children to find.

Easter week, which Christians calls Holy Week, is traditionally a holiday bringing with it lazy days with plenty of time for long breakfasts, time to talk and family games and activities. Like Moses and the Jews before their exodus from Egypt, we eat lamb at Easter and the lamb is also a symbol for Christ.

In Scandinavia people believe that witches gather together to dance in the nearest graveyard on Easter Eve.

Depending where you live signs of springtime bring us into a new season. In the north the snow is melting into small streams from the eaves, further south daffodils emerge from snow-free flowerbeds and pussy willow and catkins appear on the almost bare trees.

If you are lucky, the sun will come out and start to warm your dormant garden. Put on your wellies and go for a walk, or just sit and relax in the sunshine, which will bring new life to you and the countryside around you.

This friendly group of rabbits, lambs, hares and geese have been invited to a springtime Easter celebration, and they may even stay for the rest of the spring – perhaps even for the whole year if you like. Isn't it nice to know that when you sit down with your sewing machine, you give life to new friends?

The sun inspires the yellow of Easter, but pastel colours are also popular for this springtime celebration and have been used throughout this book. But, of course, when using the patterns to make the items in this book the choice of colour is entirely yours.

We wish you a creative and happy Easter and spring!

Best regards,

Tone Finnanger

Contents

Thank you to:

Nina, Kari, Vanessa, Torje and Matti for all their help in connection with this book.

I would also like to thank Ingrid Skaansar and Grete Syvertsen Arnstad for their wonderful support, and Kristine Steen and Karin Mundal at Cappelen for their excellent cooperation.

All photos have been taken in the old shop at the lovely Kilen gallery at Hvasser. All props which are not privately owned are supplied by Tinnies hus in Tønsberg.

Fabrics and materials

Fabrics

Fabrics with a slightly coarse weave are better for making stuffed figures than thin fine fabrics. They are easier to mould, and at the same time firmer, making a nicer shape.

Linen fabrics are used for a lot of these stuffed figures while a fine terry cloth is used for the sheep and some of the bunnies.

Linen has also been used for the clothes and as the base fabric for larger household items such as tea cosies, wall hangings, etc.

Any clothes, appliqué work and figures that are not to be stuffed, can be made from cottons, polyester cottons – in fact all kinds of fabrics.

As well as the fabric sections in department stores and specialized fabric shops, you will also find a lot of different patterned fabrics in shops that sell patchwork and quilting fabrics. You could also try curtain and upholstery shops where you will often find a good selection of checked and striped fabrics.

Making faces

The faces on many of the figures are created using a combination of paint, inkpad and embroidery. You will also need pins with different sized heads and a paintbrush.

Hair

The curly hair used on the good witches, is available in many colours in craft and hobby shops.

Fusible interfacing

Fusible interfacing is available in various thicknesses, but we use a heavyweight fusible interfacing, which is almost as thick as table cotton, and a lightweight fusible interfacing. Both have adhesive on one side and they are ironed on to fabric to bond it and give it body.

Other materials

You can buy polyester toy stuffing and layered wadding to stuff or pad the figures and other items. Collect natural materials for wreaths, and look for plywood hearts and plywood birdhouses, steel wire, pearl beads, paper, card, ribbons, raffia and model paint. These can be found in most hobby shops.

A list of shops and mail order suppliers is given after the patterns at the end of the book.

Plywood birdhouses decorate this Easter wreath.

A collection of fabrics, fabric paints and other useful items found in craft and hobby shops.

How to make a good stuffed figure

General instructions for stuffed figures and tips for getting good results.

Fabrics used for the stuffed figures in this book

- Lambs: Brown linen and terry cloth.
- Bunnies: Light or dark brown linen, or terry cloth.
- Hares: White or sand-coloured linen.
- Chickens/hens: Light or dark brown linen for the body. Terracotta linen or cotton for beaks and legs.
- Eggs: Various kinds of fabric.
- Large geese: White or sand-coloured linen for the body. Terracotta linen or cotton for beak and legs.
- Small geese: Linen or cotton for the body. Thinner fabrics for beaks and legs.
- Witches: Dark or light brown linen.
- Hearts: Various kinds of fabric.

Read more about fabrics on page 4.

Useful tools

- Fabric markers such as a fine pen with washable ink or a well-sharpened pencil to trace the pattern on to the fabric. Use light colours on dark fabrics and dark colours on light fabrics.
- A pair of small pointed fabric scissors.
- A transparent sewing machine foot will make it easier to see and follow the pattern drawn on the fabric.
- A wooden flower stick is a very useful tool for turning the fabric inside out and for stuffing the figures. Polish the end with sandpaper to avoid splinters catching in the fabric.

Method

1. Trace the pattern and sew

There are several ways of transferring the pattern, but templates made from card or acetate sheet are a good solution. Place the sheet of acetate over the pattern and draw the outline of the pieces with a waterproof pen. For card, put transfer paper between the pattern sheet and the card and trace round the outline to transfer it on to the card. If you have a scanner or photocopier, you can copy the pattern sheets and glue them on to card. If the pieces overlap, make several copies of the same sheet. Write the name of the pattern piece on the template, then cut out the acetate or card pattern very accurately with sharp scissors.

Draw round the pattern pieces on the fabric but do not cut them out until you have stitched them. For two identical pieces fold the fabric double, right sides together, and then draw the pattern. Do not place the pieces too close together. Mark all openings for stuffing or turning the fabric inside out. Most openings are marked by a broken line along the seam. If the opening is marked inside the pattern piece, there will be no seam opening. The line you draw is the stitching line. Using a 1.5-2mm

(¹⁄₁₆in) stitch length, stitch accurately round the pieces by hand or machine, see figure A.

2. Cutting out

Cut out the pieces with a narrow seam allowance, 3mm (⅛in) is enough. You should cut extra seam allowance of 7-8mm (¼in) where there are openings in the seam, see

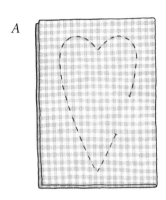

A

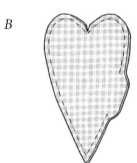

B

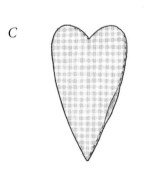

C

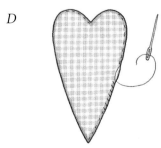

D

figure B. Where the opening for turning inside out is marked inside the pattern piece, you should cut according to the marking through one layer of fabric only.

Cut notches in the seam allowance around the pattern piece where the seam curves inwards, see figure B.

3. Turn inside out

A sanded wooden flower stick is a good tool for turning pieces inside out and stuffing. As the seam allowance is narrow, the pieces have to be turned carefully. Slide the wooden stick along the seam after turning them inside out in order to make all the shape details stand out.

4. Press

Fold in the extra seam allowance at the openings and finger press. This does not apply to the extra seam allowance at the top of the arms and legs as they will be tucked into the body. Press the pieces before stuffing them, except figures or body parts made from terry cloth, see figure C.

5. Stuffing

Insert the stuffing loosely into the figure, making sure that it does not form a lump until it is well in place. For small details like the witches' noses and thumbs, etc, shape a small piece of stuffing and push it in place before stuffing the rest of the figure.

Use the stick to push the stuffing carefully but firmly into place. Use enough padding to create a firm well-shaped figure. Some pieces, like the arms of the witches, are only stuffed in the lower part, allowing them to bend and look good once the figure has been clothed.

Terry cloth stretches more than woven fabrics, like the linen used for stuffed figures. Consequently, terry

cloth figures or figure parts should not be stuffed too firmly. Simply stuff terry cloth lambs and bunnies until you have a good shape.

There are several qualities of stuffing. A good quality stuffing should not form lumps too easily nor be too smooth, but be somewhere in between. Avoid upholstery wadding which may have lumps. Do not use layered wadding to stuff figures.

6. Sewing up

Hand sew up the openings used for turning inside out, see figure D. Where these openings are visible, for example at the side of the hearts or on the underside of the small geese, try to make the stitches as invisible as possible. If the opening curves inwards, try pulling the fabric a little, massaging the outline into shape.

Detailed instructions for making each figure are given with the relevant pattern.

Decoration on clothes

Heart patterns for decoration given on page 67.

A little extra decoration on dresses, trousers and hats will never go amiss. The decorations on the clothes for bunnies, hares and hens were made with various sewing machine embroidery stitches, so check what is available on your machine. If your machine does not do embroidery, you can sew crosses and dotted lines by hand, as shown on the witches' clothes, see pages 38–39. Hand-sewn decoration can be added after the clothes are made up. We have used three strands of embroidery thread, for the simple crosses and decorative hems on the witches' clothes.

If you are adding the decorations by machine, you will have to do this before the clothes are made up in order to reach. Instructions are given under the different patterns.

An attractive decorative touch, used together with machine or hand embroidery, is to tie a row of buttons along the bottom of a skirt using embroidery thread.

You can also add appliqué patches such as the fabric hearts on the lambs, see page 10, or the clothes of the geese, see page 30. Appliqué instructions are given on page 40. Add the appliqué after the clothes are finished and then add blanket stitches around the edge by hand.

Faces

Put off adding the face details until you have the ears, hair and hat in place. Then it is easier to see where the eyes should go.

You will need: Sewing pins with different sized heads, black fabric paint, an ink pad in a muted pink colour – old rose is best – and a brush. (You can use lipstick instead of an ink pad.)

Put roses in the cheeks by applying the colour with the brush. Dip the head of the sewing pin into black paint and stamp eyes on to the face. Dip once for each eye and clean the head after making one eye.

Noses

Noses for bunnies and hares are sewn with pink thread as shown in figure A. All kinds of thread can be used and the number of stitches depends on the thickness of the thread chosen.

Noses for sheep are sewn with black thread in a Y shape as shown in figure B.

Iron-on tape

This tape is very useful for hemming sleeves, skirts and trouser legs that are too small to be machine sewn. Before turning the garment right side out, fold up the trouser leg, skirt edge or sleeve hem, cut lengths of tape, push into the fold and iron to bond.

A

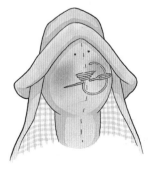

B

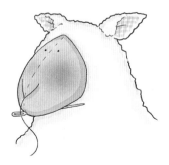

Lambs

Pattern given on pages 66 and 67.

These lambs, made from terry cloth, are very cuddly. They bring a touch of spring to your sofa at Easter and will stay for the rest of the year. They make a delightful present for a new baby.

A medium terry cloth in a light colour, such as off-white, beige or sand, is good for lambs. Use a finer weight terry cloth to make the small lambs stitched together as a garland, shown on page 12, as the parts of the body will be easier to turn inside out.

This is how you do it

Read the general instructions for making stuffed figures on pages 6–7.

Trace the pattern for the large lamb head and body matching the dotted lines at points A-A and B-B.

Fold the terry cloth double, right sides together, trace the pattern on to the fabric and cut out two body pieces with a 5mm (¼in) seam allowance. Cut two pieces of linen fabric and trace the face outline on each. Sew the face pieces to the body, see figure A. Press seams open.

Place the body right sides together, and sew around as shown in figure A, starting and ending at the tops of the legs. Fold the body the other way so that the front and back seams match and sew the legs, see figure B.

Trim seam allowances and turn inside out through a leg opening.

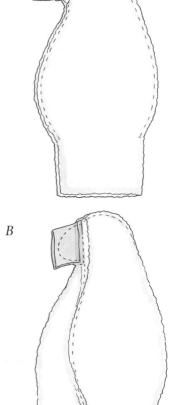

A

B

Fold a piece of terry cloth double, right sides facing, trace the pattern for the arms twice, sew the side seams and then cut out with a 5mm (¼in) seam allowance.

Fold a piece of linen fabric double, trace a pair of hands and a pair of feet, sew around the pieces leaving the ends open and cut out. Turn arms, hands and feet right side out.

Stuff the hands and feet well and tack across the openings to keep the padding in place. Fold in the seam allowance at the lower end of the arms and insert the hands so that the part outside the dotted line sticks out. Stitch them on, see figure C.

Stuff the body as described on page 7 but do not stuff the tops of the legs if you want the lamb to sit.

Fold in the seam allowance at the end of each leg and insert the feet. Sew around the openings gathering them to fit around the feet.

Push a little stuffing into the arms, fold in the seam allowances at the tops and tack them on to the body.

Place a piece of towelling and a piece of ear lining fabric, right sides together. Trace the ears from the pattern, sew around them, cut out and turn them inside out. Fold in the seam allowance at the bottom of each ear and fold the bottom edge in half. Stitch to the head, see figure D.

Paint the face and stitch the nose as described on page 8.

Add an appliqué heart on the front as described on page 40 and tie a bow round the neck, see figure E.

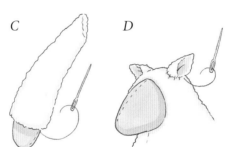

C *D*

E

Garland of lambs

Use the small lamb pattern to make a cute garland of lambs. The arms of the small lambs stand straight out from the body, making them different from the large lambs. However, they are sewn on in the same way. Instead of making separate legs run a line of stitching between them to divide them. This makes the figures hang better. Sew three finished lambs together to form a garland. Stitch a small plastic or brass ring for hanging on the back of the hand at each end.

You could hang up single lambs so that they look like they are flying...

This terry towelling lamb looks at home in the bathroom, propped up against the pile of hand towels.

The Easter bunny is also well known. Rabbits reproduce so rapidly that they are symbols of fertility heralding the new life spring brings, and look how cute they are sitting here in all their finery.

Bunnies

Patterns given on pages 68, 69 and 70.

You will need:

- Dark or light brown linen for the body
- Fabric for lining ears
- Fabric for clothes
- Stuffing
- Embroidery threads and fabric paints for the face and clothes

This is how you do it

Note that the bunnies and their clothes come in two sizes.

Body

Read the general instructions for making stuffed figures on pages 6–7.

Fold the linen double and trace round the patterns for the body (once) and arms and legs (twice). Sew around the pieces leaving ends open, see figure A.

Place the linen fabric and the ear lining fabric right sides together, trace the ear shape and sew around it, leaving an opening, see figure B.

Cut out all the pieces, turn inside out and press. Stitch the ear opening. Stuff the body, arms and legs.

Insert the legs into the end of the body and sew up the opening to fasten the legs. Then stitch the arms to the body and the ears, lining side down, to the head, see figure C.

Make the face and stitch a nose as described on page 8. If the bunny is to wear a hat, you may want to postpone adding the face until the hat is in place.

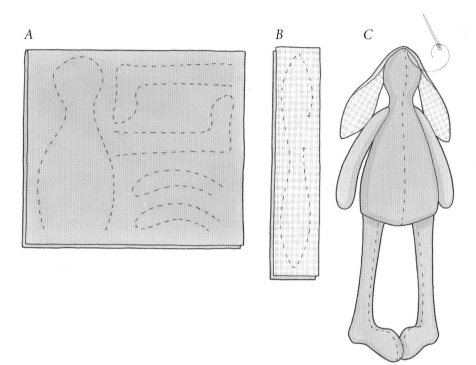

A *B* *C*

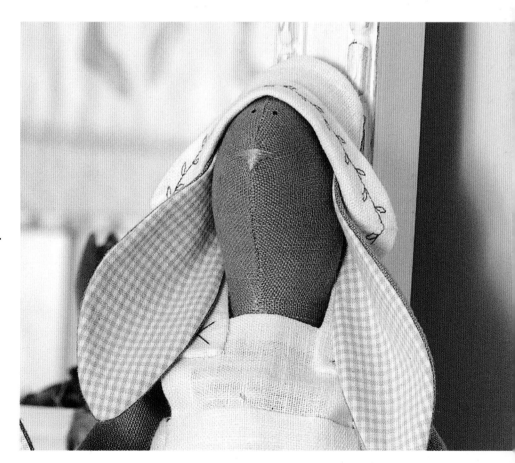

Clothes

Machine embroidery to decorate the clothes has to be done before the pieces are sewn together. See decorating clothes on page 8.

Pantaloons

The pantaloons are worn by the bunnies, page 15; hares, page 20; and witches, page 36. The instructions given below apply to all three figures. You will find the correct pattern on the same page as the patterns given for each figure.

Fold the fabric in half and place the straight edge of the pattern piece on the fold. Cut out two pieces for the pantaloons, adding extra seam allowance at the waist and at the bottom of the legs.

Place the two pieces with right sides together, and sew the centre seams, see figure A.

If you want machine embroidery at the bottom of the legs, fold up the hem and use the embroidery to fasten it before you sew the leg seam. Make sure the embroidery is on the right side, see figure B. If you do not want any embroidery, or if you are adding hand-sewn decorations, leave the hems until you have sewn up the trouser legs.

Match the centre seams and sew the leg seams, see figure C.

Turn and press the pantaloons and fold in the seam allowance around the waist. If you have not yet hemmed the legs, press up the seam allowance, insert iron-on tape and press to hold as described on page 8. Then add the embroidery.

Put the pantaloons on the figure, making small tucks at the waist if necessary. Stitch the pantaloons to the body, see figure D.

A

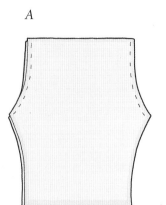

B

C

D

Pinafore dress

This dress is also worn by the bunnies, page 15; hares, page 20; and witches, page 36. The instructions given below apply to all three figures.

The measurements for the dress skirt are given below. The patterns for the bib and straps can be found on the same page as the patterns given for each figure.

Skirt measurements:
These correspond to one skirt piece.
Large bunny and hare – 20.5cm (8in) wide, 18cm (7in) deep.
Small bunny and hare – 14.5cm (5¾in) wide, 13cm (5⅛in) deep.

Witch – 20.5cm (8in) wide, 20.5cm (8in) deep.

Cut two skirt pieces to the measurements given above and a bib according to the pattern for the figure. Add seam allowances at the top and bottom of the skirt pieces, and all around the bib.

Press in the seam allowance at the top and on each side of the bib and hold them in place using iron-on tape, see page 8.

With right sides together place the bib centrally on one of the skirt pieces and sew it on, see figure E.

Press the bib up.

E

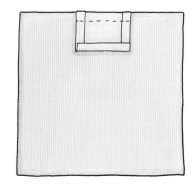

The small goose from page 34 is also a great accessory for other figures. Here the bunny plays with a goose on wheels.

Add any machine embroidery at this stage. An embroidered heart has been machined on the skirt just below the bib, as described on page 8, see figure F. Place the dress skirt pieces with right sides together and sew together up the sides. Press side seams open and then turn up the hem along the bottom and fix using iron-on tape. Press down the seam allowance at the top without fixing with tape.

Bunnies also look sweet made of terry cloth, like these charming bathroom bunnies.

Turn the dress inside out. Hand or machine embroider along the bottom of the dress, if you wish.

Straps

Fold the dress fabric in half and place the pattern for the straps along the fold. Cut out two straps and sew along the long and one short edge, see figures G and H. Turn the straps inside out and press.

Put the dress on the figure. Stitch two tucks at the front of the dress, one on each side of the bib, and two at the back, so the skirt fits the body. Place the stitched ends of the straps on the front of the bib and attach by hand sewing crosses or buttons, see figure I. Cross the straps at the back, tuck the open ends inside the skirt and stitch to hold.

Hat

This hat is also worn by the geese, page 30; the instructions apply to both. The pattern is on the same page as the patterns for the figure.

Fold the fabric for the hat double with right sides together, trace the pattern and sew around it, leaving an opening, see figure J.

Cut out, turn inside out and press. Fold the half of the hat with the opening into the other half and press, see figure K.

Embroider around the inner edge of the hat before pressing the brim up at the front and down at the back, see figure L. Pull the hat firmly on to the head and add a few stitches at the neck and on each side.

Make the face if not already done.

F

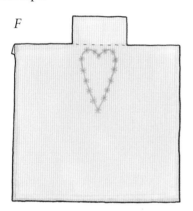

G

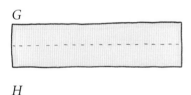

H

I

J

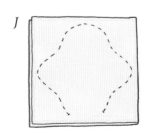

K

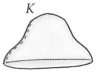

L

Hares

*Patterns given on
pages 68, 69 and 70.*

You will need
- White or sand-coloured linen for the body
- Fabric for lining the ears
- Thin steel wire for the ears
- Fabric for clothes
- Stuffing
- Fabric paints and embroidery threads for the face and clothes

---

According to Anglo Saxon legend, the Easter hare was originally a bird whose wings were frozen. The goddess of spring, Eostre, freed it from the ice and transformed it into a hare but the hare continued to lay eggs and became a symbol of fertility and new life. These hares will probably not lay eggs, but they will make a nice decoration for both Easter and spring.

This is how you do it

Hares and bunnies are made in the same way except for their ears. Make up the body and clothes for the small and large hare as described for small and large bunnies on pages 15–19.

Ears

Place a piece of linen fabric and a piece of ear lining fabric with right sides together. Trace two ears from the pattern and sew around the edges, see figure A. Cut out and turn the ears inside out. Fold in the seam allowance at the bottom of each ear and press them. Shape two pieces of steel wire into approximately the shape of the ears and push them into each ear. The shaped wire should be longer than the ears, so that about 2cm (¾in) of each end of the wire stick out of the ears.

Push the wire ends into the stuffed head of the hare and tack the ears on to the head, see figure B. Bend the tops of the ears over as shown.

A

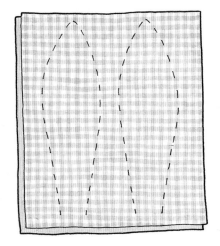

B

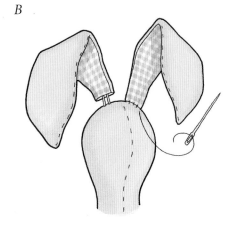

Flowerpot hares

Flowerpot hares are made by sewing a body with ears, but without arms and legs. Tack the body across the bottom after stuffing it, and put it into a flowerpot. Decorate the top of the pot with twigs held in place around the edge with a glue gun.

Thread beads on to thin steel wire and wind them around the twigs.

Decorate the pot with a heart, tracing round the pattern given on page 67. Paint the outline of the heart on the pot using a fine paintbrush. Then stamp the dots using the large and small heads of pins. Start by placing the large dots evenly along the painted line and then surround these dots with six smaller dots.

Hens

Pattern given on page 71.

You will need:

- Light or dark brown linen for the body
- Terracotta linen for beak, comb and legs
- Fabric for the dungarees
- Stuffing
- Fabric paints for the face and embroidery threads for the clothes

The pattern for the hen on this page has been enlarged to 120% on a photocopier. The hens opposite are the size of the pattern. The larger pattern makes details easier to sew.

This is how you do it

Read the general instructions for making stuffed figures on pages 6–7.

Fold the brown linen double, right sides together, and trace the pattern for the body. Cut away enough fabric so that you can sew on two pieces of terracotta linen where the beak will be, and trace the beak. Sew around the body and beak, see figure A. Cut out, and turn the body inside out.

With the brown linen double, trace the pattern for the wings and sew around, see figure B.

Fold the terracotta linen double, right sides together. Trace the patterns for the comb and wattle and sew around, see figure C.

Cut out and turn all the parts inside out. Stuff the body and wings as described on page 7. Fold in the

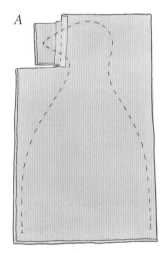

A

B

C

So, which came first? The chicken or the egg – that is the question. Perhaps a hare laid the first Easter egg? As an Easter symbol the hen is likely to be linked to the egg – and an Easter without hens is quite unthinkable!

seam allowance around the opening on the comb, and stuff the comb and wattle using a stick to get into the corners. Sew up the wattle opening.

Cut a piece of terracotta linen 21cm x 14cm (8½in x 5½in) for the feet. Press down 1cm (½in) at the top and bottom, see figure D.

Place the fabric flat with the folded edges facing down, then fold up 3cm (1¼in) at the bottom and fold the top edge down so that the pressed edges meet, with the folds now facing up, see figure E. Trace the feet so that the dotted line on the pattern matches the opening between the folds and sew around, see figure F.

If you are not too fond of small fiddly details the hen pattern can successfully be enlarged, as done here with the hen in the patchwork dungarees.

D

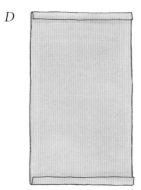

E

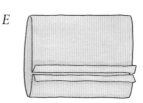

F

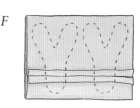

G

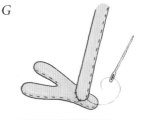

Cut out, turn inside out and stuff the feet as described on page 7.

Make the legs following the instructions for the straps given on page 19. Fold in the seam allowance around the opening and stuff the legs using a wooden stick. Tack the open ends of the legs on to the feet to cover the foot openings, see figure G.

Place the other ends of the legs into the bottom of the body. Sew across the opening so that the legs are fastened. Stitch on the wings. Fold the wattle in half and stitch it under the beak. Sew the comb to the head and paint the face as described on page 8, see figure H.

H

Dungarees for hens and geese

The dungarees are also worn by the geese, page 30. The instructions given below apply to both figures. You will find the pattern on the same page as the patterns for the figure.

Fold the fabric in half and place the pant pattern on the fold. Cut out two dungaree pant pieces, adding extra

seam allowances at the waist and the bottom of the legs. Cut out a bib piece with extra seam allowances round three sides.

Place the two pant pieces with right sides together, and sew up one side along the curved edge as shown in figure A.

Turn and press the seam allowance across the top and each side of the bib. Insert lengths of iron-on tape and iron to hold.

With right sides facing sew on the bib across the centre seam of the dungaree pants. Fold down the waist hem and press with the bib up. Embroider a heart by hand or machine over the seam as described on page 8, see figure B.

Fold the pants with right sides together and sew along the other curved edge (see figure A).

Fold the dungaree pants the other way so that the seams now match each other and sew the legs, see figure C.

Press seams open. Fold up the seam allowance at the bottom of each leg, insert iron-on tape and press to hold. Turn inside out and put the dungarees on the figure.

Make two tucks at the front, one on each side of the bib and two at the back so that the dungarees fit at the waist. Stitch the tucks to hold.

Sew on the straps as described on page 19. Fasten the straps with crosses or buttons at the top of the bib. Cross them at the back, insert inside the waist and stitch to hold.

Fold a big tuck at the outside bottom edge of each dungaree leg and stitch to hold, see figure D.

The patchwork dungarees are made from 4.5cm (2in) patches plus seam allowance. The pattern has been enlarged to 120% on a photocopier.

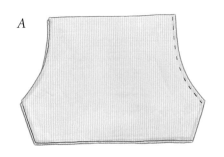

A

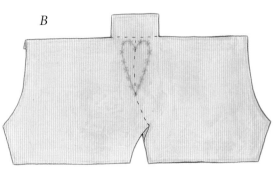

B

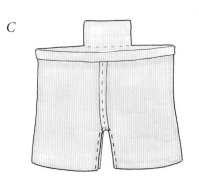

C

D

Eggs

Pattern given on page 72.

Pattern given on page 72.

You will need
- Fabric for the egg
- Stuffing
- A piece of string

A   B   C

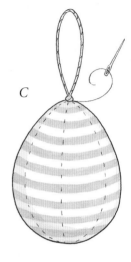

This is how you do it

Read the general instructions for stuffed figures on pages 6–7.

The egg pattern comes in two sizes. Fold a piece of fabric in half, quarters and then thirds to create six layers. Fasten the layers together with pins. Trace the pattern for the egg on the top layer and cut out six egg sections through all the layers. Make sure the seam allowance is the same width all around the six patterns. Remove the pins, place egg sections 1 and 2 with right sides together and sew along one edge, see figure A. Then place egg section 3 with egg section 2, right sides together, and sew along edge. Continue until you have joined all six egg sections. Finally place egg section 6 against section 1 and sew together, leaving an opening in the middle to turn the egg inside out, see figure B.

Turn the egg inside out and stuff it firmly before stitching up the opening. Tie a loop of string and sew it on to the end of the egg if you want to hang it up, see figure C.

You can sew on pearl beads or buttons as decorations. Use a long needle and stitch through the egg.

Flat eggs for wreaths

Flat eggs also come in two sizes, to use on small and large wreaths.

Fold a piece of fabric double with right sides together. Trace the pattern for the egg and sew around it. Cut out the egg and cut an opening for turning it inside out through one layer of the fabric. Turn it inside out and press the egg. The egg should be well stuffed to make the edges nice and even. You can gently press the egg flat with an iron after stuffing, before tacking up the opening on the back.

Glue the eggs round a wreath with a glue gun.

Eggs are perhaps the most important symbol of Easter, and there is no Easter without them. Fill a bowl with large eggs made from beautiful fabrics, or hang smaller eggs on a bunch of budding twigs.

Geese

Pattern given on page 73.

You will need

- White or sand-coloured linen for the body and wings
- Terracotta linen for the beak, legs and feet
- Fabric for clothes
- Raffia strips for the bow
- Fabric paints for the face and embroidery threads for the clothes

Geese often pop up at Easter – just take a look at old picture postcards. Their funny appearance makes them so lovable!

This is how you do it

Read the general instructions for stuffed figures on pages 6–7.

The smaller geese are made from the pattern given on page 73. The pattern has been enlarged to 120% on a photocopier for the large goose.

The body with beak and wings of the geese are made in the same way as for the hens on page 24.

Fold the terracotta linen double and trace the feet and leg patterns. Mark extra seam allowances at the bottom of the legs as given on the pattern. Sew around the feet and up the side seams of the legs including the seam allowance, see figure A. Cut out the pieces, cut a cross opening on each foot as marked on the pattern.

Turn the feet and legs inside out. Fold in the seam allowance at the bottom of the legs before stuffing them. Stuff the feet. Tack the openings of the feet closed and then sew the legs on to the feet so that they conceal the openings, see figure B.

Insert the legs in to the bottom of the body and sew up the opening fastening the legs. Sew on the wings.

Make the dungarees, and dress the figure as described for the hens on page 27. Make the hat and fasten to the head as described for the bunnies on page 19.

Create the face as described on page 8 and tie the raffia strips into a bow around the neck, see figure C.

A

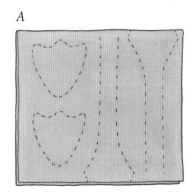

B

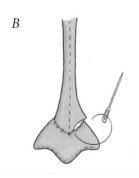

C

This goose has an appliqué heart decoration on the dungarees. Use the heart pattern given on page 67, and follow the instructions for appliqué given on page 40.

Small geese

Pattern given on page 74.

Pattern given on page 74.

You will need

- Linen fabric for the body
- Thin cotton fabric for beak and legs
- Stuffing
- Stick and raffia strips for bow *or* 4 buttons and string
- Fabric paints for the face

This is how you do it

Cut a length of fabric sufficient for two bodies; cut a strip 10cm x 2cm (4in x ⅞in) from the centre of one long side. Cut a 3.5cm x 10cm (1½in x 4in) strip of beak fabric and stitch to fill the space, see figure A.

Fold the fabric double, right sides together, and trace the body pattern, matching the beak seam with the line on the pattern. Sew around leaving an opening at the bottom, see figure B. Cut out, turn inside out and press. Stuff and sew up the opening, leaving a small space to insert a stick. Make a face as described on page 8.

Fold a piece of leg fabric double, trace the leg pattern and sew around leaving an opening, see figure C. Cut out, turn inside out and press. Sew up the opening. Thread the goose on to the stick and tie on the legs. Add a few stitches to fasten them to the body, see figure D. Tie a raffia bow around the goose's neck.

A

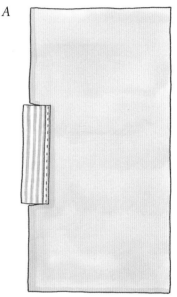

B

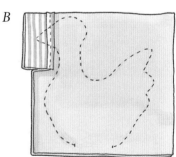

C

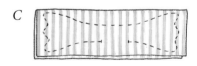

D

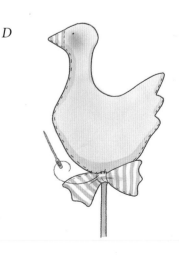

Stick a flock of geese in a flowerpot for a simple and amusing Easter decoration. For a goose on wheels sew two buttons on each side and tie a length of string around its neck.

Good witches

Pattern given on pages 74 and 75.

Witches are part of the Easter tradition in Scandinavia, even if they do not have the best reputation. On Easter Eve all witches fly off to a party and if they are good witches – like these shown here – they are bound to have a very nice time!

You will need
- Light brown linen for the body and arms
- Fabrics for clothes, stockings and shoes
- Toy hair
- Stuffing
- Small goose, see page 34
- Fabric paints for the face and embroidery threads for clothes

This is how you do it

Body
Read the general instructions for stuffed figures on pages 6–7.

Sew a strip of the shoe fabric along the long edge of a strip of the stocking fabric. Press seam open then fold the joined fabric in half,

matching seams and with the right sides together. Trace the leg pattern so that the line marking on the pattern is along the seam line between the fabrics and sew around, leaving the tops open, see figure A.

Fold the skin fabric double and trace the body and arm patterns and sew around leaving openings. Cut out the pieces adding extra seam allowance at the openings. Turn inside out, press and stuff the body, legs and arms as described on page 7. Only the lower part of the arms should have padding, so they hang nicely and can be folded up.

Tuck the seam allowance at the top of the legs into the opening at the bottom of the body and stitch up the opening so that the legs are fastened to the body. Stitch the arms to the body, see figure B.

A

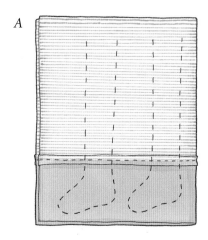

B

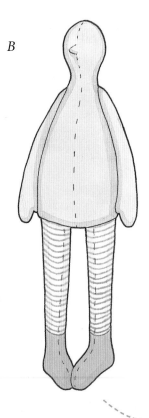

C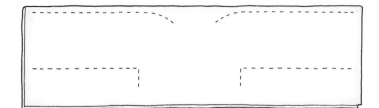

D

Clothes

Any decorative stitching on the clothes should be done before making up as described on page 8.

Make up the pantaloons as described on page 16.

Make the shirt pattern template by placing the centre line on the fold of a piece of paper. Trace round the outline, open out and use this to cut out a pattern piece from card or acetate. Fold the shirt fabric double, with right sides together, trace round the pattern and sew around leaving openings, see figure C.

Cut out the shirt and use iron-on tape to hem the seam allowance at the opening for the neck. Press up the seam allowance at the end of each sleeve without bonding tape then turn the shirt inside out.

Put the shirt and pantaloons on the figure and tack the lower edge of the shirt to the waist edge of the pantaloons. Run a line of gathering stitches round the ends of the sleeves and pull up to fit the sleeves around the wrists and then fasten off.

Sew the pinafore dress as described on page 16 and put the dress on the figure over the shirt and pantaloons.

Hat

Sew a strip of lining fabric to a strip of hat fabric. Fold the joined fabric in half, right sides together, matching the seam. Trace the hat matching the line on the pattern with the seam, and sew around leaving an opening, see figure D. Cut out and turn the hat inside out. Push the lining into the rest of the hat and press. Fold the brim up in the front and press to keep it in place. Stuff the hat to make it stand up well.

Fix some toy hair to the sides of the head and pull the hat tightly on the head. Fasten the hat to the head with a few invisible stitches at the back and on each side.

Create the witch's face as described on page 8. Twist one of the arms around inside the sleeve so that the thumb points up and out before you place the hand to the face and stitch it on. Make a small goose without legs as described on page 34. Tack the goose to the witch and stitch the other hand to the goose to make it look as if she is holding it under her arm, see figure E.

E

Hare appliqué

Pattern given on pages 76 and 77.

The appliqués are brushed with fabric paint to give them an appealing finish. It is not at all difficult and makes the decoration more coherent.

The pattern pieces consist of a hare head, teapot with separate lid and a mug and they can be combined in several different ways. The pictures on the following pages will give you ideas of how these motifs can be put together or you can create your own designs.

This is how you do it

The pattern pieces for the appliqué decorations are reversed because the outlines are traced on the wrong side of the fabric. When the figures are turned round, they will match the decorations shown in the pictures.

Place double sided iron-on interfacing on the wrong side of the fabric and press to bond. Remove the backing paper.

Trace the outlines of the pattern pieces on to the wrong side (the glue side) of the bonded fabric and cut out. Place the pieces on a sheet of paper, card or acetate film with the right side up.

Look at the pictures of the appliqué decorations to see where the painted effect is placed on the figures. Dip a dry brush into the fabric paint and dab off the excess on a piece of paper, leaving only a little paint on the brush. Brush the paint on to the pieces, moving the brush quickly back and forth. Leave to dry

then repeat the process if the effect is too weak.

If the edges of the fabric have frayed a little where the piece has been painted, wait until the paint is dry and then trim the edge with sharp, pointed scissors.

Place the appliqué pieces on the background fabric, starting with the lowest piece and iron them on.

The head of the hare is outlined with a neat running stitch using a contrasting thread. The labels are outlined in the same way. Blanket stitch around the mugs and teapot by hand or with a sewing machine. Add a line of running stitches for the coil of 'steam' as shown in the pattern.

The words on the labels have been sewn as simply as possible using long straight stitches. Draw the words using a washable marker pen before stitching them. You could practise first on an acetate sheet and then transfer the words on to the fabric.

Decorate the faces on the figures as described on page 8.

Bright eyed, friendly hares peep out from teapots and mugs, asking if it's teatime. On the following pages you will find instructions to make the tea cosy and potholders for you to appliqué, and more ideas for you to decorate your Easter table.

Potholders

Measurements for the pattern pieces are given in the text.

You will need

- Fabric for the front and loop
- Lightweight fusible interfacing
- Lining fabric for the back
- Wadding
- Fabrics for the appliqué
- Fabric paints for the face and embroidery threads

This is how you do it

Iron fusible interfacing to the wrong side of the front fabric pieces to get a firm base for the appliqué.

Cut out a piece of front fabric, a piece of lining fabric and two pieces of wadding each measuring 17cm x 23cm (6¾in x 9in), adding seam allowances. Cut a strip of fabric measuring 4cm x 11cm (1¾in x 4⅓in) without seam allowance for the loop. Press just under 1cm (½in) to the wrong side along each of the long sides, see figure A. Then fold the strip in half, matching the edges of the folds, and sew along the long side, see figure B.

Place two layers of wadding on the wrong side of the fabric lining and zigzag stitch round the edge to fasten the wadding to the fabric.

Appliqué the decoration on to the front of the fabric as described on page 40. Place the appliquéd fabric piece and the lining with right sides together. Place the loop between the fabric and the lining at the top of the potholder and sew round the edge, leaving an opening at the bottom for turning it inside out. See figure C.

Trim any excess seam allowance and turn the potholder inside out. Fold in the seam allowance at the opening and sew it up. Press the potholder and then sew a seam about 6mm (¼in) in from the edge with the sewing machine, see figure D.

A

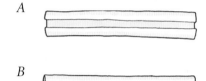

B

C

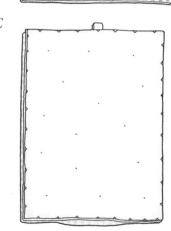

D

*Charming
potholders ready
for action on hot
teapot handles.*

Tea cosy

Pattern given on page 78.

You will need:

- Fabric for the tea cosy and the loop
- Lining fabric
- Heavyweight fusible interfacing *or*
- Wadding with lightweight fusible interfacing
- Fabrics for appliqué, see page 4
- Fabric paints for the face and embroidery threads

This is how you do it

Trace the tea cosy pattern so that the dotted lines between A and B match each other. Fold the fabric, lining and interfacing in half and place the centre line of the pattern on the folds of the fabrics, see figure A.

Cut out two pieces of fabric, two pieces of lining and four pieces of heavyweight interfacing or two pieces of lightweight interfacing and two pieces of wadding according to the pattern, adding seam allowances.

Iron two layers of heavyweight interfacing to the wrong side of each of the fabric pieces and sew around with zigzag stitches to keep the layers in place.

If you are using wadding first iron lightweight fusible interfacing to the wrong side of each of the two fabric pieces. Then add the wadding to each piece and sew around with zigzag stitches to keep them in place.

Appliqué the hare and tea pot decoration on one of the fabric pieces as described on page 40.

Place each fabric piece right sides together with a lining piece and sew them together along the curved bottom edge, see figure B. Trim to leave about 7–8mm (⅜in) seam allowance along the curve to make a neat edge at the bottom of the cosy.

Make a loop in the same way as you did the loops for the potholders on page 42.

Open out the fabric and lining pieces and place the two parts of the tea cosy with right sides together. Make sure the seams along the curved bottom edges match. Place the loop between the two layers of fabric at the top and sew around leaving an opening for turning inside out in the lining, see figure C.

Cut off the excess seam allowance around the tea cosy. Press the seam allowance between the lining and the fabric towards the lining.

Turn the tea cosy inside out and sew up the opening.

Push the lining into the tea cosy. The seam allowance between the fabric and the lining makes a decorative edge at the bottom of the tea cosy.

Press the tea cosy, making sure the bottom border edge is even.

A

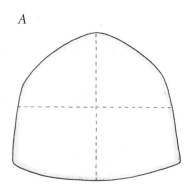

B

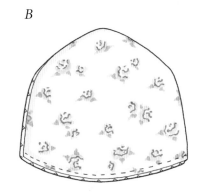

C

44

A happy teapot motif cheers up a simple tea cosy. The tea cosy is made of light blue linen with a floral lining which forms a border at the bottom.

tid for te?

This tea cosy in beautiful pink linen has a floral tea pot appliqué creating a romantic look which signals it is springtime.

The bags from page 62 can be used as napkin holders. This size fits breakfast napkins.

47

Bird house egg cosies

Pattern given on page 78.

You will need

- Fabric for the bird house and contrast fabric for the roof edges
- Lining fabric
- Heavyweight fusible interfacing
- Button and stranded embroidery thread

You can use lightweight interfacing and wadding instead of heavyweight interfacing as described on page 44.

This is how you do it

Iron heavyweight fusible interfacing on to the wrong side of the fabric for the bird house. Trace round the pattern and cut out two bird houses. Trace and cut out two pieces of lining fabric. Place each lining piece right sides together with a fabric piece and sew along the curved edge, see figure A. Open out the fabric and the lining pieces and place the two parts with right sides together. Sew around the edge leaving the pointed roof edge open, see figure B.

Turn the egg warmer inside out through the opening. Push the lining into the bird house fabric and press the egg cosy.

Cut a strip of fabric of 3.5cm (1½in) wide with a length equal to

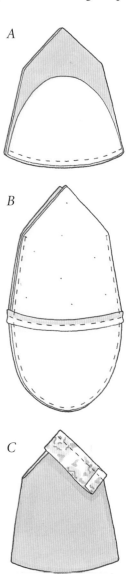

48

one of the sides of the roof plus a seam allowance at one end. Fold in the seam allowance, place the strip along one of the roof sides with right sides together and stitch, see figure C. Fold the strip over the house roof edge so that the roof strip is about 1cm (½in) wide, fold under the other long edge and hem it on the other side, see figure D. Cut another strip the same width but with seam allowances at both ends. Fold in the seam allowance at each end and stitch, see figure E, then fold over the edge as before and finish by folding up the edge and hemming it.

Tie a button to the front of the bird house with embroidery cotton.

D

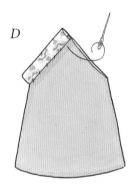

E

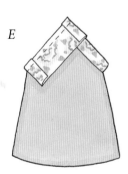

Traditionally we decorate eggs for Easter. These hard boiled eggs are simply decorated with stick-on decoupage roses.

Decorative glasses

Plain straight-sided glasses become very decorative if you cover them in fabric. Cut out a piece of fabric to fit the height and circumference of the glass with seam allowances. Press in an edge at the top, leaving a lip to drink from, and bottom and fix with iron-on tape, see page 8. Before wrapping round the glass you can sew a decorative heart in the middle of the fabric strip. Pull the fabric tightly around the glass and put two marks at the top and two marks at the bottom where the two sides meet. Fold the strip with right sides together, matching the points and sew between them along the edge. Cut off surplus seam allowance, press open then turn the fabric inside out and pull it on to the glass.

Wall hanging with rag hares

Pattern given on page 76.

Four newly laundered rag hares are hanging on the line, ready for Easter. Half clothes pegs and dresses made from pleated fabric are sewn on to give a three-dimensional effect.

This is how you do it

The background panel of the wall hanging is made from off-white linen with a sand-coloured linen border. Linen can pull out of shape so iron lightweight fusible interfacing on the back to make it easier to work with.

Add seam allowances to the measurements given for the panel and borders strips. The panel in off-white linen measures 70cm x 31cm (27½in x 12¼in).

Run a line of stitches about 5cm (2in) in from one long edge using a contrast colour thread. This will be the washing line. Cut two strips of sand-coloured linen, 70cm x 6cm (27½in x 2¼in) and sew to the centre panel, see figure A. Cut two more strips, 43cm x 6cm (17 x 2¼in) and sew on to each side, see figure B.

Appliqué the heads, arms and legs of the four hares as described on page 40, remembering that the pattern pieces are reversed. Place each head with one ear on the washing line. Trace the outline of the dress on to the background using a washable marking pen to help place the arms and legs. Do not sew on the

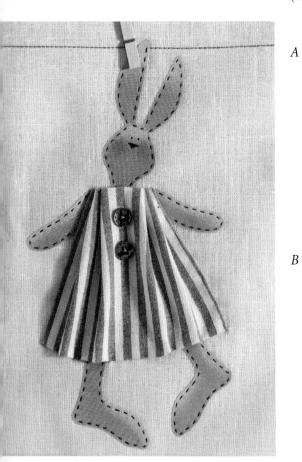

A

B

dresses, buttons and clothes pegs yet.

Cut out the backing fabric and the wadding to measure 82cm x 43cm (32¼in x 17in) plus seam allowances.

Place the bordered panel over the backing, with wrong sides together and sandwiching the wadding. Pin round the edge. Machine embroider just inside the border to hold the layers in place. Trim any excess fabric or wadding so that you have neat straight edges. If necessary sew a zigzag seam around the outer edge to hold the layers in place.

Bind the wall hanging with bias tape, or use an attractively patterned fabric as we have done here. Cut lengths of 4cm (1⅝in) wide fabric strips and join them together to make a piece that goes all round the picture. Starting in one corner, place the strip with the right side facing the front of

C

D

the wall hanging. Stitch about 6mm (⅜in) in from the edge, see figure C.

When you reach the corner, stop sewing about 6mm (⅜in) from the edge, see figure D. Fold the strip as shown in figure E, before continuing down the next side. When the strip is sewn all around the picture, fold it over and hem round on the reverse, see figure F. Press the hanging.

Cut out pieces of fabric about 11cm x 15cm (4¼in x 6in) for the dresses, adding a seam allowance all round. Fold in the allowances and insert iron-on tape along the top and bottom hems to hold. Make a couple of pleats at the top on each side of the head and pin to the backing fabric at the shoulders and down the sides. Adjust pleats, then sew to the backing fabric. Leave the bottom loose, catching it in one or two places if necessary. Sew on two buttons.

Split the clothes pegs in two and tack the half pegs on. You can use some glue to fasten them securely.

Sew plastic or brass rings on the back of the picture to hang it up.

E

F

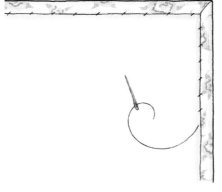

Easter hearts

Pattern given on page 79.

Padded hearts

Make some cute Easter hearts from patchwork or plain fabric decorated with appliqué and embroidery.

Read the general instruction for stuffed figures on pages 6–7.

To make patchwork hearts, sew together patches to get a piece of fabric large enough for the heart pattern. The patches are 4.5cm (2in) square plus a seam allowance.

If you make large hearts from a plain thin fabric, iron lightweight fusible interfacing on to the wrong side first to strengthen it.

Fold the fabric double, with right sides together, and trace the heart pattern. Leaving an opening for turning inside out, sew round the outline and cut out.

For small hearts and hearts for

decorating wreaths, sew all round the outline, then cut an opening through one layer of fabric at the back.

Turn the heart inside out and stuff it as described on page 7. Sew up the opening. Appliqué a hare's head to the right side of the heart, see page 40. Add a raffia bow and a small stuffed heart to finish. Fasten a piece of string at the top to hang up.

The hall has been decorated for Easter.
Patchwork hearts in toning colours are
used to decorate a twig wreath.

Twig hearts

Use a length of thick steel or zinc
wire to make a heart shape. Wind
some twigs around the heart
holding them with thin, dark steel
wire. Finally, thread some pearl
beads on to fine steel wire and twist
it around the heart for decoration.

Twig hearts entwined with beads
make simple and beautiful
decorations all through the year.

59

Cards

Pattern given on page 79.

The cards are cut from sheets slightly larger than A4 and measure 32cm x 16cm (12¾in x 6¼in) folded in half to make them square. You can buy cards this size, but they are also easy to make. The gift tag is 24.5cm x 6cm (9¾in x 2½in).

This is how you do it

The backing panel and the largest egg are made from fabric and attached directly to the card with iron-on fusible tape, see page 40.

Do not use too hot an iron or the card will wrinkle. Sew a zigzag edging around the panel and the egg with a sewing machine.

Cut out the hare's head and the small egg from card. You can draw a decorative line of stitches around the head with a pen. Cut out and glue on a little nose. Make the rest of the face as described on page 8. Glue the hare's head and the small egg on the card with double-sided tabs, then tie a raffia bow and glue it on the hare. Make a hole through both layers of the card with a hole punch. When you have written the card, you can tie it on with a piece of ribbon.

The gift tag is also made from card. The egg has been glued directly on the tag, while the head has been fastened with a double-sided tab.

Send an Easter card to friends and family. If you've got time, you can make them yourself.

Sweet bags

Measurements for the pattern pieces are given in the text.

It is traditional to give eggs at Easter. Some are made of chocolate others are made of card and filled with sweets. You could make a small bag and fill it with eggs and other goodies as a present. The bags can be used for storing other things afterwards, such as paper napkins, or cotton wool for the bathroom. And, of course, they can always be used just as bags.

This is how you do it

Cut out two pieces of fabric, two pieces of lining and four pieces of heavyweight fusible interfacing each measuring 17cm x 25cm (6¾in x 9⅞in) plus seam allowances.

Iron heavyweight fusible interfacing to the wrong side of each fabric piece and zigzag stitch round the edges to keep the layers together.

A layer of wadding can be used as an alternative to heavyweight fusible interfacing, if so iron lightweight fusible interfacing on to the wrong side of the fabric and stitch wadding to the interfaced side of the fabric.

Cut two strips of fabric 3.5cm x 25cm (1½in x 9⅞in) plus seam allowances for the handles. Fold each strip lengthwise with right sides together. Sew across one short side and up the long side, see figure A.

Turn the handles inside out and stuff them using a wooden stick.

Place the fabric pieces with the interfacing/wadding right sides together with the lining pieces. Mark 5.5cm and 7cm (2¼in and 3in) in

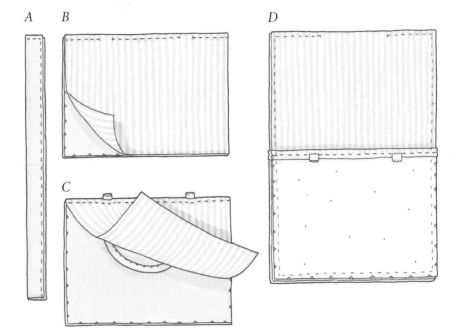

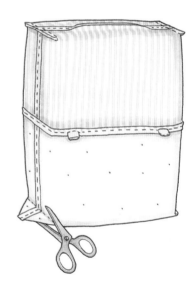

from each side on one of the long edges of each piece and sew leaving two openings for handles in each part, see figure B. Push the ends of the handles through the openings between the fabric and lining. Stitch across the handles, see figure C.

Open out the fabric and lining, place the two bag parts with right sides together and sew round the edge, leaving an opening in the lining for turning inside out, see figure D.

Mark 4cm (1½in) up from each corner on the short sides of the fabric and the lining. Fold the corners so that side and bottom seams match, and sew across the corner crossing the marks. Cut off the corners outside the seam, see figure E.

Turn the bag out and stitch up the opening. Push lining into the bag and press the edges with the iron to get a good shape, see figure F.

On a plain bag, appliqué a hare's head as described on page 40 and tie on a raffia bow. Make a patchwork bag from 4.5cm (2in) square patches, plus a seam allowance. Make up the bag as described above.

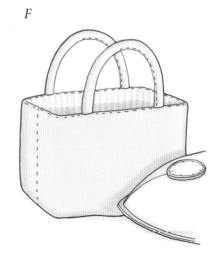

Easter eggs

We often buy ready-made Easter eggs in the stores, but they are quite easy to make.

In hobby shops you can buy decorated and plain card eggs made in two halves that fit together. You can cover these plain or decorated eggs with fabric. First paint the eggs white and when dry then cover them in fabric using either decoupage glue or hobby glue. Cut off the excess fabric, leaving about 1cm (½in) to fold and glue inside the edge.

Of course the eggs can also simply be painted in different colours, and then decorated with the heart design from the flowerpot hares as shown on page 23, for example.

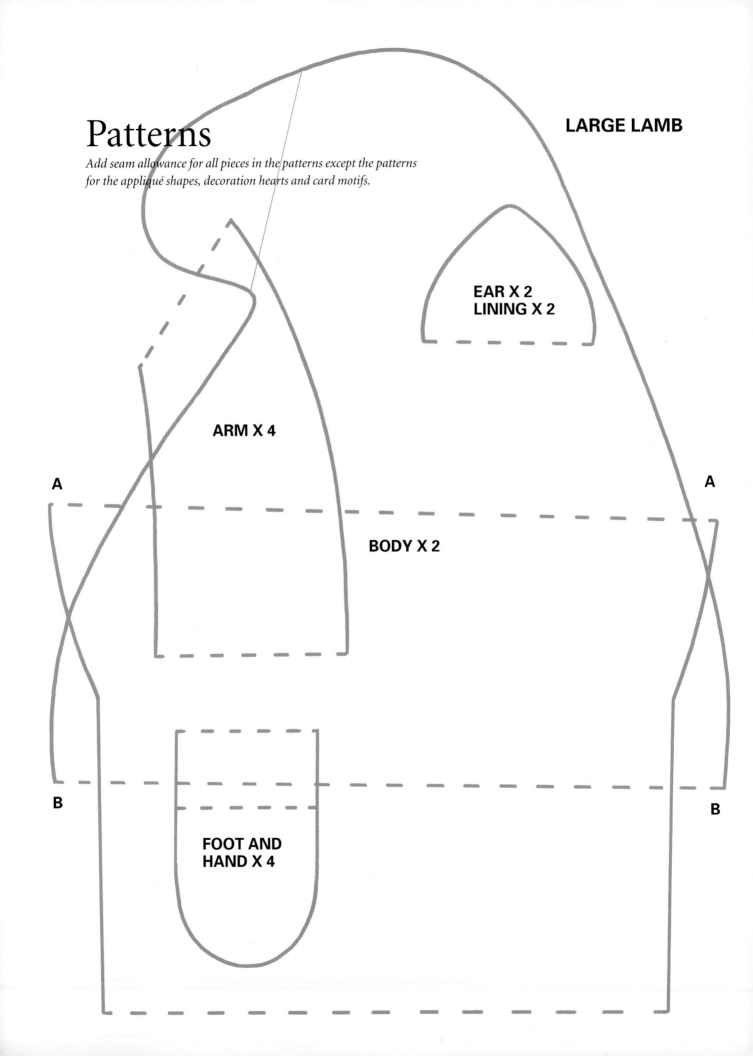

Patterns

Add seam allowance for all pieces in the patterns except the patterns for the appliqué shapes, decoration hearts and card motifs.

LARGE LAMB

**EAR X 2
LINING X 2**

ARM X 4

A   A

BODY X 2

B   B

**FOOT AND
HAND X 4**

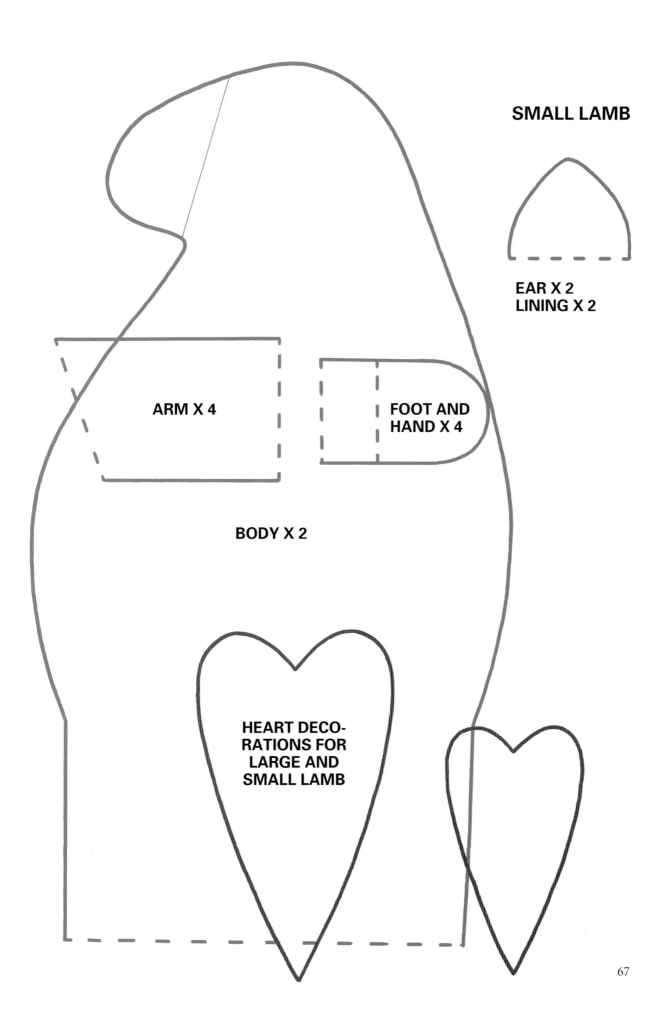

SMALL LAMB

EAR X 2
LINING X 2

ARM X 4

FOOT AND
HAND X 4

BODY X 2

HEART DECO-
RATIONS FOR
LARGE AND
SMALL LAMB

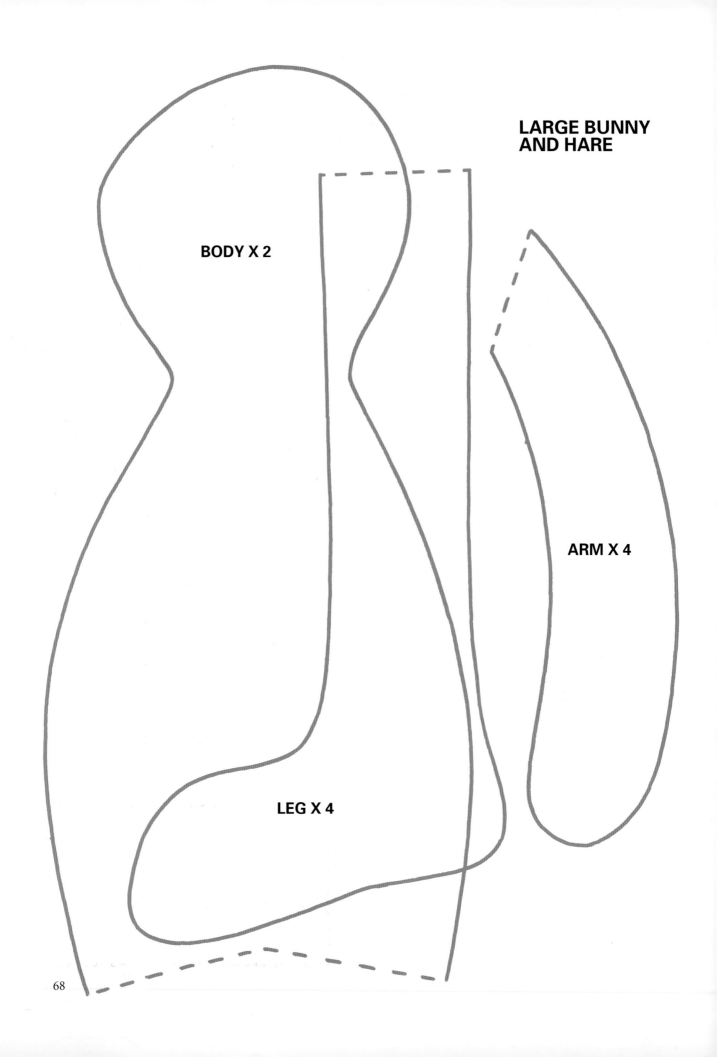

LARGE BUNNY
AND HARE

BODY X 2

ARM X 4

LEG X 4

68

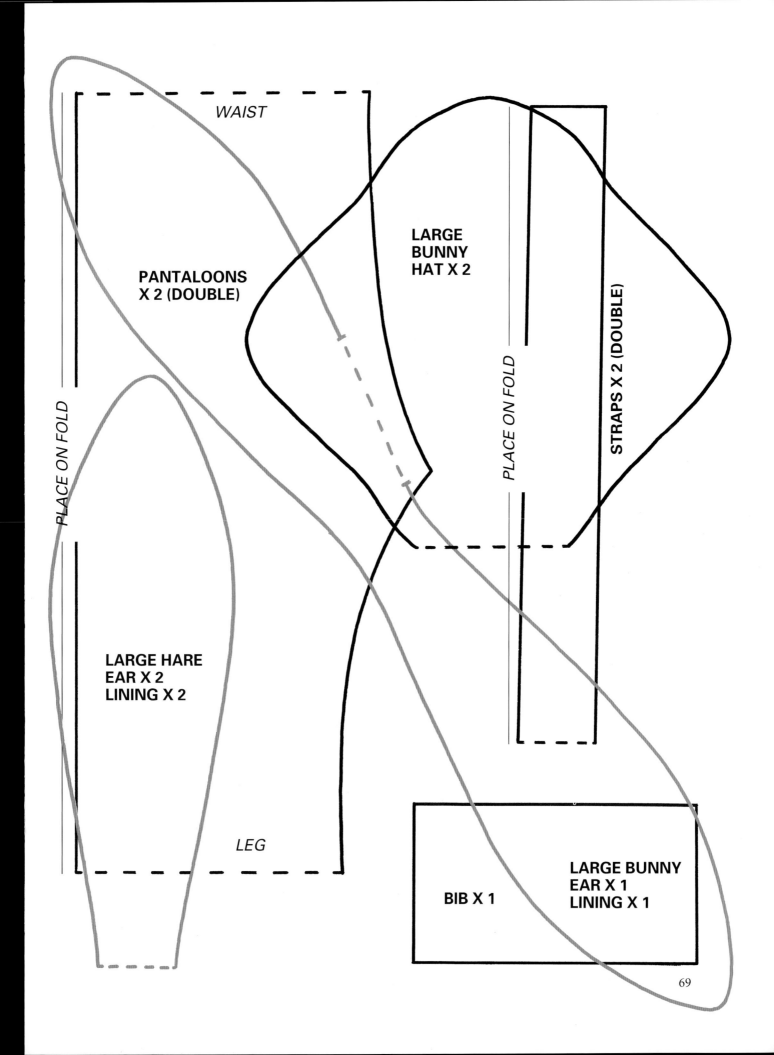

WAIST

PANTALOONS
X 2 (DOUBLE)

PLACE ON FOLD

LARGE
BUNNY
HAT X 2

STRAPS X 2 (DOUBLE)

PLACE ON FOLD

LARGE HARE
EAR X 2
LINING X 2

LEG

BIB X 1

LARGE BUNNY
EAR X 1
LINING X 1

69

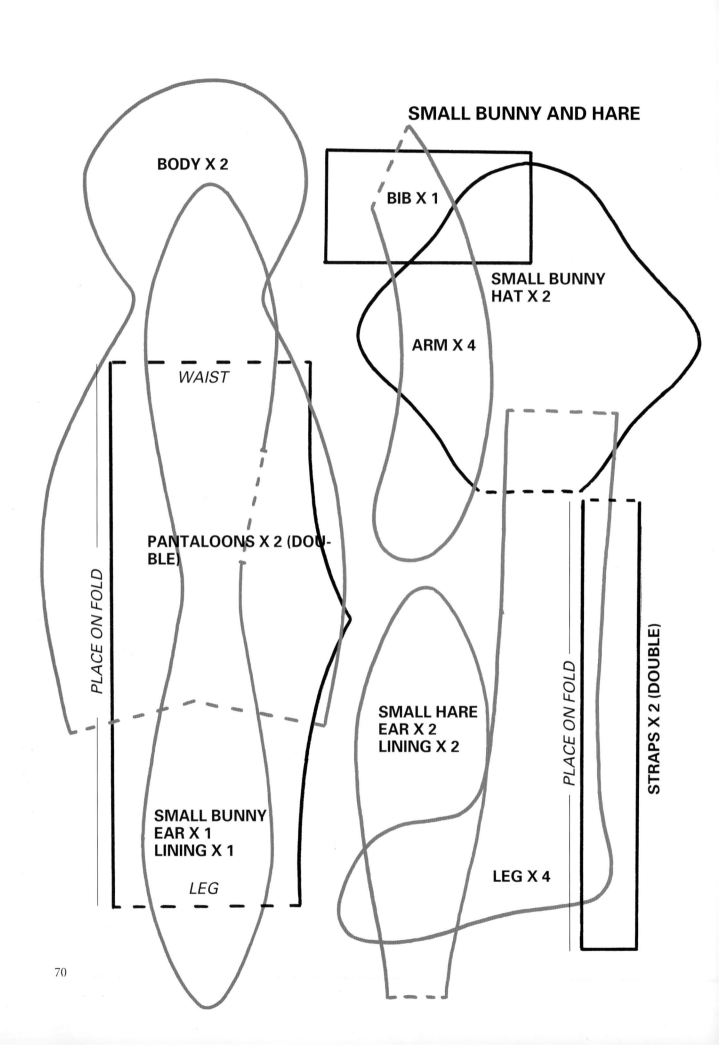

SMALL BUNNY AND HARE

BODY X 2

BIB X 1

SMALL BUNNY
HAT X 2

ARM X 4

WAIST

PLACE ON FOLD

PANTALOONS X 2 (DOU-
BLE)

SMALL HARE
EAR X 2
LINING X 2

PLACE ON FOLD

STRAPS X 2 (DOUBLE)

SMALL BUNNY
EAR X 1
LINING X 1

LEG

LEG X 4

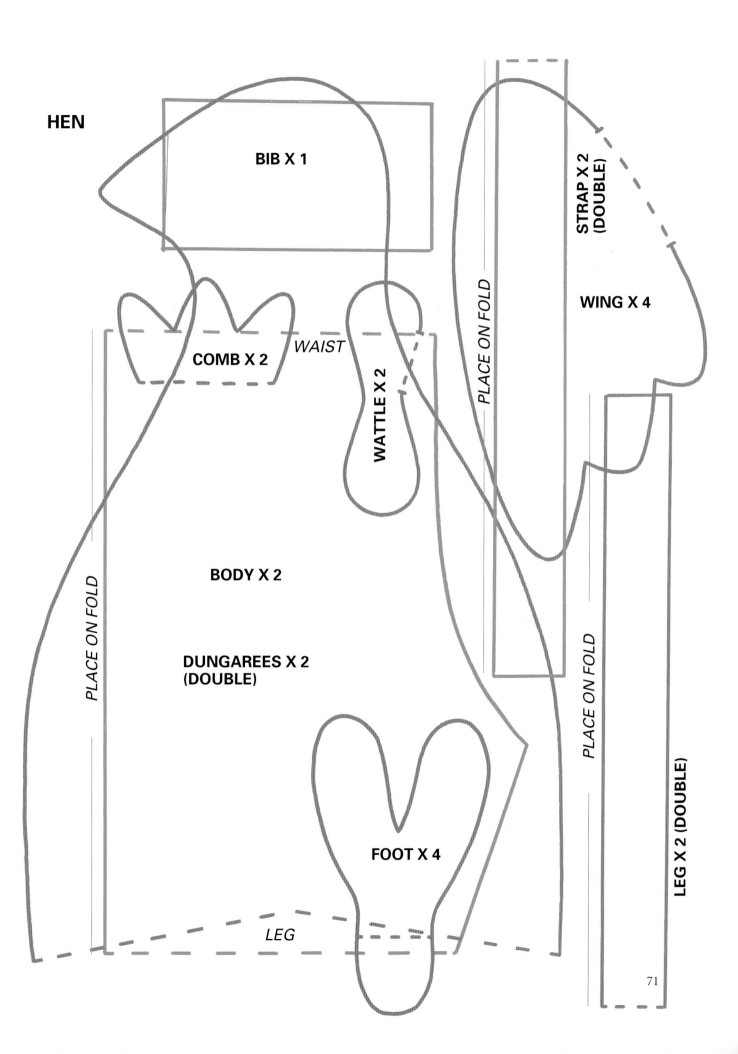

HEN

BIB X 1

COMB X 2

WAIST

STRAP X 2
(DOUBLE)

WING X 4

WATTLE X 2

PLACE ON FOLD

BODY X 2

PLACE ON FOLD

DUNGAREES X 2
(DOUBLE)

PLACE ON FOLD

FOOT X 4

LEG

LEG X 2 (DOUBLE)

71

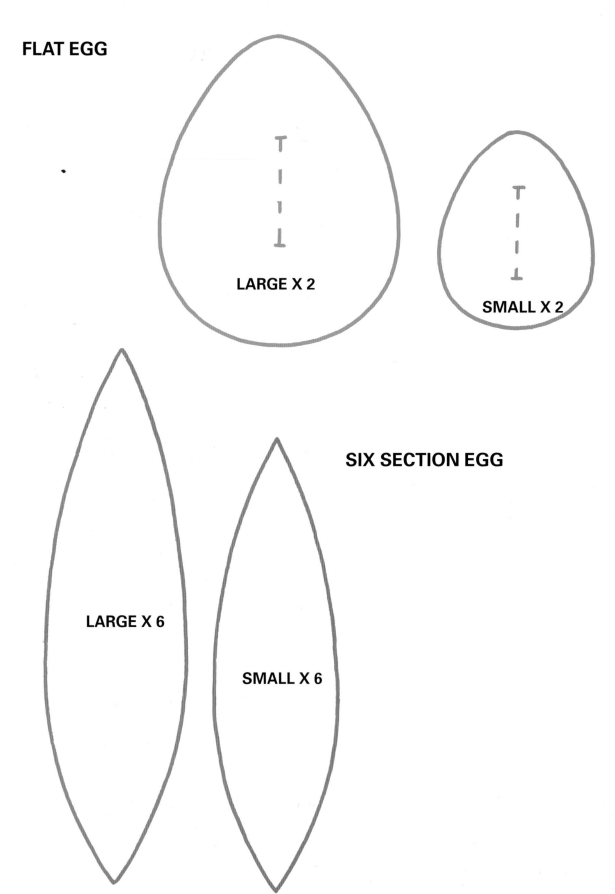

FLAT EGG

LARGE X 2

SMALL X 2

SIX SECTION EGG

LARGE X 6

SMALL X 6

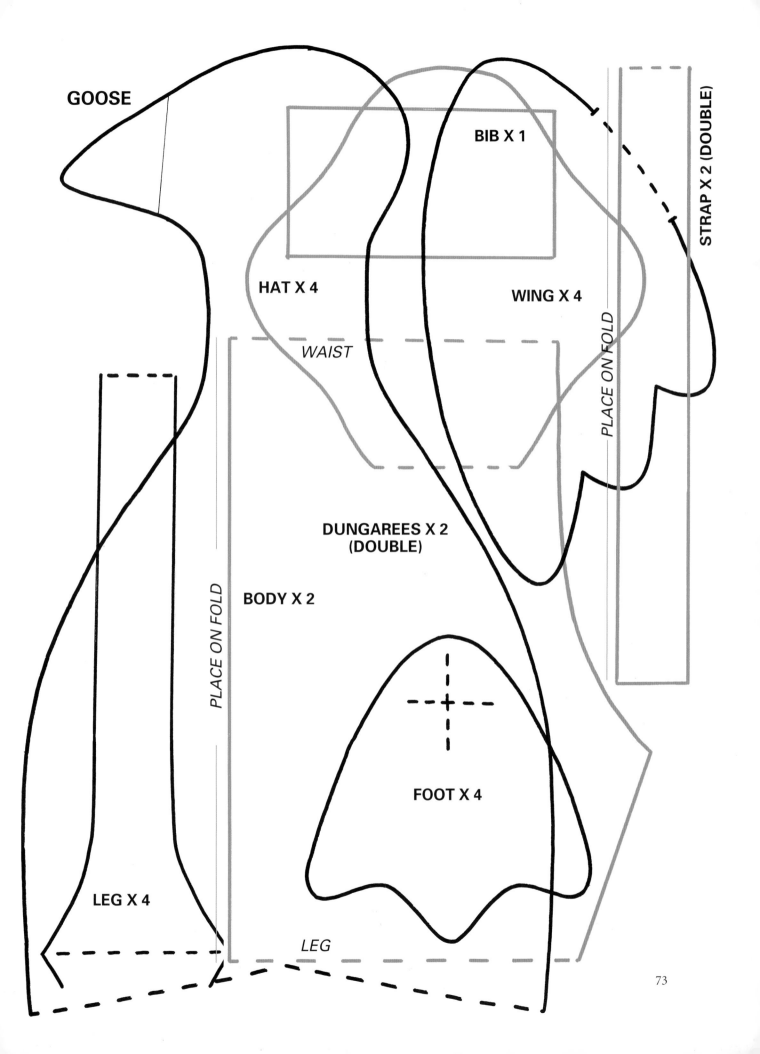

SMALL GOOSE

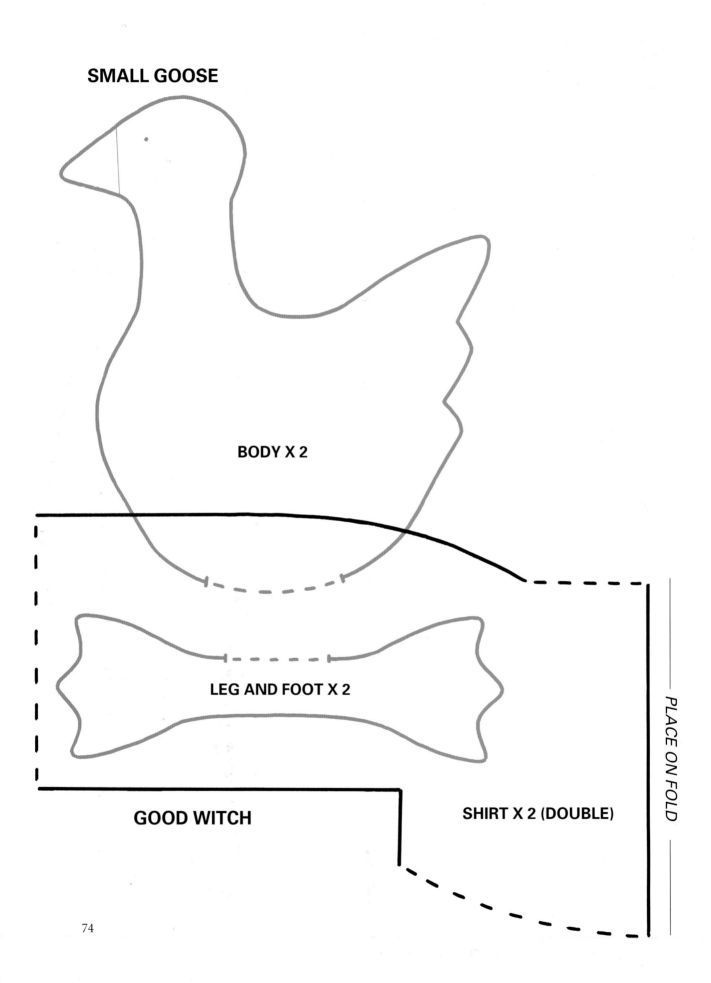

BODY X 2

LEG AND FOOT X 2

GOOD WITCH

SHIRT X 2 (DOUBLE)

PLACE ON FOLD

GOOD WITCH

WAIST

PLACE ON FOLD

PANTALOONS X 2 (DOUBLE)

BODY X 2

ARM X 4

HAT X 2

LEG X 4

LEG

75

tea?

time

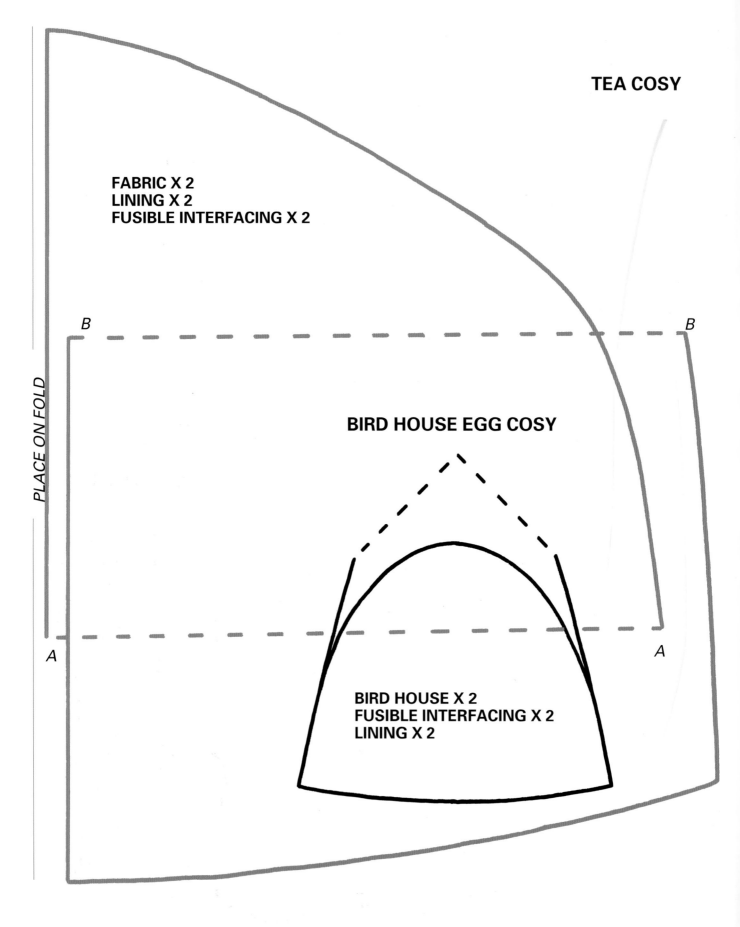

TEA COSY

FABRIC X 2
LINING X 2
FUSIBLE INTERFACING X 2

PLACE ON FOLD

B

B

BIRD HOUSE EGG COSY

A

A

BIRD HOUSE X 2
FUSIBLE INTERFACING X 2
LINING X 2

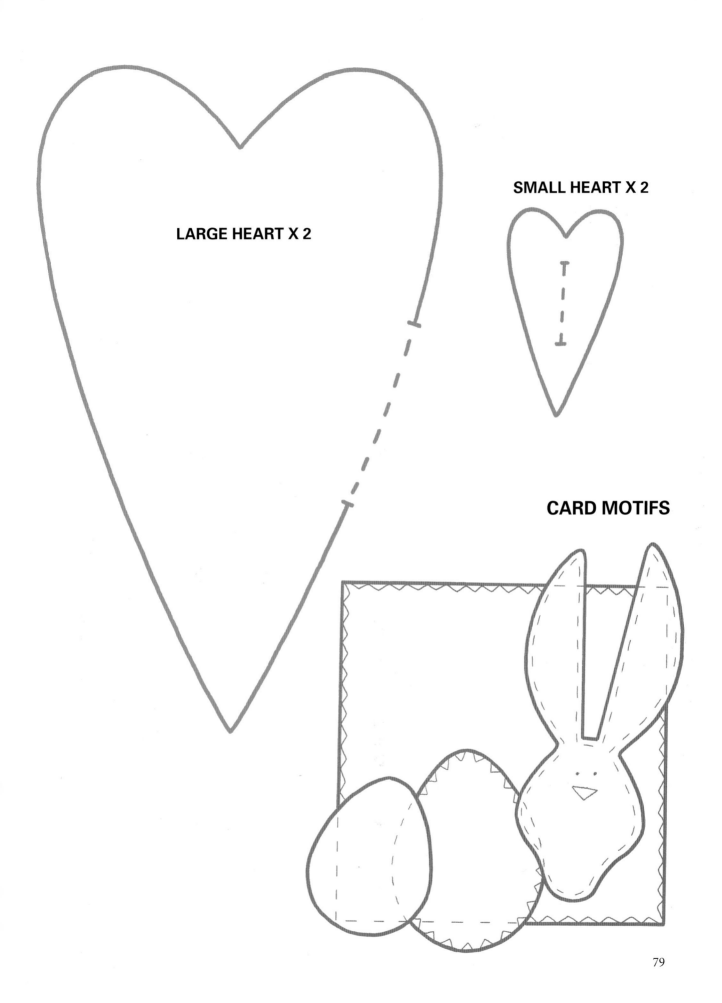

LARGE HEART X 2

SMALL HEART X 2

CARD MOTIFS

Suppliers

UK
Quilting materials
- The Bramble Patch
  West Street
  Weedon
  Northants NN7 4QU
  Tel: 01327 342212

- The Cotton Patch
  1285 Stratford Road
  Hall Green
  Birmingham B28 9AJ
  Tel: 0121 702 2840
  www.cottonpatch.net

Threads
- Coats Crafts UK
  PO Box 22
  Lingfield House
  McMullen Road
  Darlington
  Co Durham DL1 1YQ
  Tel: 01325 394237
  www.coatscrafts.co.uk

- DMC Creative World
  Pullman Road
  Wigston
  Leicester L18 2DY
  Tel: 0116 281 1040
  www.dmc/cw.com

Beads and sequins
- Ells & Farrier
  20 Beak Street
  London NW2 7JP
  Tel: 0207 629 9964

Fabrics
- Ragbags
  3 Kirkby Road
  Ripon
  N Yorkshire HG6 2EY
  www.ragbags.net

- Willow Fabrics
  95 Town Lane
  Mobberley
  Cheshire WA16 7HH
  Tel:0800 056 7811
  www.willowfabrics.com

- Fabric Flair Ltd
  The Old Brewery
  The Close
  Warminster, BA12 9AL
  Tel: 0800 716851

General embroidery supplies
- Voirrey Embroidery Centre
  Brimstage Hall
  Wirral L63 6JA
  Tel: 0151 342 3514

USA
Threads
- Coats and Clark USA
  PO Box 12229
  Greenville
  SC29612-0229
  Tel: (800) 648 1479
  www.coatsandclark.com